Moving Leadership Standards Into Everyday Work

Descriptions of Practice

SECOND EDITION

Karen Kearney, Editor

Printed in the United States of America.

10 9 8 7 6 5 4 3 2 1

ISBN: 978-1-938287-33-6

eISBN: 978-1-938287-34-3

Library of Congress Control Number: 2015953120

Suggested citation: Kearney, K. (Ed.). (2015). *Moving leadership standards into everyday work: Descriptions of practice* (Second Edition). San Francisco, CA: WestEd.

WestEd — a nonpartisan, nonprofit research, development, and service agency — works with education and other communities throughout the United States and abroad to promote excellence, achieve equity, and improve learning for children, youth, and adults. WestEd has more than a dozen offices nationwide, from Massachusetts, Vermont, and Georgia to Illinois, Arizona, and California, with headquarters in San Francisco.

WestEd operates the California Comprehensive Center (CA CC), 1 of 15 Regional Comprehensive Centers funded by the U.S. Department of Education. The CA CC provides intensive technical assistance to the California Department of Education. More information about the CA CC is available at http://cacompcenter.org.

WestEd books and products are available through bookstores and online booksellers. WestEd also publishes its books in a variety of electronic formats. To order books from WestEd directly, call its Publications Center at 888-293-7833, or visit us online at http://www.WestEd.org/bookstore.

For more information about WestEd:

Visit http://www.WestEd.org

Call 415-565-3000 or toll free 877-4-WestEd

Write WestEd, 730 Harrison Street, San Francisco, CA 94107-1242

This work was supported in part by the California Comprehensive Center through funding from the U.S. Department of Education, PR/Award Number S283B120012. It does not necessarily reflect the views or policies of the U.S. Department of Education and one should not assume endorsement by the Federal Government.

CHIEF EXECUTIVE OFFICER	EDITORIAL DIRECTOR	PUBLICATIONS MANAGER
Glen Harvey	Joy Zimmerman	Danny S. Torres
CHIEF PROGRAM OFFICER	**DESIGN DIRECTOR**	**COMMUNICATIONS SPECIALIST**
Sri Ananda	Christian Holden	Tanicia Bell
CHIEF POLICY & COMMUNICATIONS OFFICER	**DESKTOP PUBLISHER**	
Max McConkey	Fredrika Baer	

Contents

Acknowledgments

Moving Leadership Standards Into Everyday Work: Descriptions of Practice (Second Edition) is a significant update to the original volume published in 2003. The collaborative project was led by the California Commission on Teacher Credentialing (CTC), with the California Department of Education (CDE); technical assistance support was provided by Karen Kearney and Heather Mattson, Educator Excellence co-leads in the California Comprehensive Center (CA CC) at WestEd.

Special thanks go to the following education leaders for generously sharing their time and expertise as members of the Descriptions of Practice Panel, which was charged with revising the descriptions of practice to reflect the newly updated California Professional Standards for Education Leaders (CPSEL): Margaret Arthofer, Ardella Dailey, Bendta Friesen, Lisa Gilbert, Margaret Harris, Janette Hernandez, Gary Kinsey, Akida Kissane Long, Pamela Mari, Christopher Maricle, Carlye Olsen, Nancy Parachini, Renee Regacho-Anaclerio, Eileen Rohan, Nancy Sanders, Ron Taylor, and Steven Winlock.

Panelist participation was supported by the following agencies and organizations: Association of California School Administrators; California Association of Professors of Education Administration; California School Board Association; California State University Channel Islands; California State University East Bay; California State University Pomona; Curriculum and Instruction Steering Committee of the California County Superintendents Educational Services Association (Kern County Superintendent of Schools; Placer County Office of Education); Fresno Pacific University; Leadership Institute at Sacramento County Office of Education; Los Angeles Unified School District; Principal Leadership Institute at University of California Los Angeles; Resourcing Excellence in Education at the University of California Davis; San Lorenzo Unified School District; Whittier Unified School District; and Yuba City Unified School District.

Additional support for the panel was provided by Gay Roby and Sarah Solari Colombini from CTC, Barbara Murchison from CDE, and Libby Rognier from CA CC at WestEd.

Funding to support educator participation in the statewide update panel, document design, and limited printing was provided through AB1476, Title II A — Teacher and Principal Training and Recruiting. Additional support for convening, panel facilitation, and writing was provided by the CA CC at WestEd, funded by the U.S. Department of Education. Editing and design for the document were provided by WestEd.

Introduction for Descriptions of Practice

Leadership effectiveness is well documented as a critical lever for achieving positive education results. In fact, research confirms what practitioners and others in education have long known: Strong, focused leadership at all levels of the education system is critical to ensuring the continuous improvement of student outcomes and school success. Effective leadership is essential in setting direction, developing people, engaging communities, and creating conditions for successful teaching and learning.

In short, highly skilled leaders are crucial to student learning and well-being. But what does good education leadership look like? Research indicates the qualities of effective education leadership, but the field is calling for more detailed descriptions of what those qualities look like in practice.

Overview of the California Professional Standards for Education Leaders and the Descriptions of Practice

The California Professional Standards for Education Leaders (CPSEL) identify what an administrator must know and be able to do in order to demonstrate effective and sustained leadership. In doing this, the six broad standards, and the specific elements within each of them, serve as a foundation for administrator preparation, induction, professional learning, and evaluation in California. Taken together, the standards describe the major areas for development and support of administrators if they are to become effective education leaders over the course of their careers.

The Descriptions of Practice (DOP) expand on the CPSEL by detailing key expectations in each standard and, for that standard, mapping what related research-based practice would look like at different points along a developmental continuum. The continuum reflects the growth of principals and other education administrators as they progress from being emerging managers to becoming strategic and collaborative leaders whose efforts result in improving student learning and well-being. Like the CPSEL, the DOP apply to all types of education administrators — at the local, regional and state levels — and are written to be adaptable for district- and site-level purposes, as well as for induction programs, coaches, candidates, and district sponsors. While many educators assume informal or ad hoc leadership roles, and while distributed leadership is a consistent theme throughout the DOP, both the CPSEL and the DOP are intended for use with or by individuals serving in formal administrative positions.

History of the California Professional Standards for Education Leaders and the Descriptions of Practice

The CPSEL have been part of California's structure for preparing and supporting education leaders since 2001, when they were adapted from the national Interstate School Leaders Licensure Consortium (ISLLC) Standards for School Leaders to fit California's priorities and context. The standards have been widely used since their inception. But as the California education context has continued to evolve, the education community has recognized the need to refresh the standards to ensure that they remain relevant and useful, reflecting an updated perspective on teaching and learning, with emphasis on 21st-century expectations for leaders, current priorities for schooling, and the needs of California's widely diverse students. In October 2013, the Commission on Teacher Credentialing (CTC) and the California Department of Education (CDE) jointly convened a panel charged with updating the standards.

The panel revisited the CPSEL to clarify expectations for today's administrators. The newly refined CPSEL, approved by the CTC in February 2014, reflect an increased emphasis on equity, access, opportunity, and empowerment for all members of the school community. However, they maintain the same basic footprint of the original standards, broadly emphasizing six major leadership areas: (1) Development and Implementation of a Shared Vision, (2) Instructional Leadership, (3) Management and Learning Environment, (4) Family and Community Engagement, (5) Ethics and Integrity, and (6) External Context and Policy. This continuity helps educators, policymakers, and programs align the updated CPSEL with current local and state policies, national leadership standards, research, and evidence-based practices.

While the general CPSEL footprint remains the same, the updated standards have a new organizational structure conceived to clarify the intent of each standard and to help to organize and define key areas of leader actions within the standard. This new structure describes the work of an education leader at three levels of specificity: at the broadest level is the *standard*, which identifies expectations for effective practice; at the next level are the *elements* of the standard, which are key areas of leader action within the standard; and at the most detailed level are *example indicators of practice*, which show how an education leader might demonstrate the element or standard within her or his practice.

Because the CPSEL are the conceptual and structural foundation for the DOP, the DOP needed to be updated to ensure their continued alignment with the standards. In October 2014, CTC and CDE convened a panel for that purpose, with its members representing a broad spectrum of educators, including practicing leaders at the site and district levels, county office of education staff, and program directors from institutions of higher education. In updating the DOP, the panel reviewed the updated CPSEL and the original DOP, as well as research studies, professional literature, and other examples of national, state, and district standards for administrators.

Purposes — Using the Descriptions of Practice

Like the original descriptions of practice, the updated DOP were developed to enhance the usefulness of professional standards for education leaders, specifically of the CPSEL. They do so by explaining the intent of each standard's individual elements and depicting what those elements look like across a continuum of practice — from practice directed toward a standard to practice that exemplifies the standard. Used with the CPSEL, these descriptions provide common concepts, language, and examples that, together, can serve various and sometimes overlapping purposes. For example, they can serve as

- a starting point for developing credentialing criteria or assessments,
- a guide for planning leadership preparation, induction, or professional learning,
- a basis for clarifying performance expectations, and
- a mirror for an administrator's self-reflection and professional goal-setting.

Given the context-specific nature of leadership, the DOP are neither intended nor suited to serve as prescriptions of practice or as a summative evaluation. Specifying how a leader might demonstrate achievement of a particular standard is a matter of local dialogue and agreement between, for example, the administrator and employer or induction candidate and credential program sponsor.

As written, the DOP are a useful formative assessment tool that can serve as one of multiple measures in an administrator supervision-and-evaluation system, but they should not be used as a stand-alone summative evaluation instrument. However, they can be used to guide the development of evaluation tools. If a district were interested in developing a fair and legally defensible administrator evaluation strategy based on the DOP, additional work would need to be done, for example, formulating a rating lower than the current lowest level on each DOP continuum in order to represent very poor performance, or even non-performance.

Structure — A Developmental Continuum of Practice

The DOP include descriptions of practice for each element of the six CPSEL. For each element, the descriptions are laid out in a four-part continuum that illustrates increasing levels of an administrator's knowledge, skills, and application, based on the example indicators of practice outlined in the CPSEL. From left to right, the four levels of the continuum show how an educator might progress from being an administrator with fundamental skills to becoming a highly accomplished leader, in relation to a particular element of a given standard.

Administrators whose practice is **directed toward the standard** have basic knowledge, skills, and attitudes that enable them to carry out their work activity by activity, with each segment independent from the others. They may be engaged in "starter" activities that will eventually lead to the results they seek, but in some instances their efforts may not be strategic or productive. At least initially, these administrators tend to keep leadership roles to themselves or a very limited number of others.

Administrators whose practice **approaches the standard** have an emerging strategic vision, enabling them to see how activities work together and to understand the leadership actions necessary to generate results. They initiate and carry out action that builds on patterns of success and lessons learned from past activities. These administrators increasingly engage staff and stakeholders in planning and team action focused on shared teaching and learning goals.

Leaders whose practice **meets the standard** are able to execute vision-driven action by capitalizing on knowing what needs to be done, how to do it, and why it should be done. They build the leadership capacity of others by engaging the staff and broader community in cooperatively working toward shared goals and opportunities that result in increasing staff and student growth and well-being.

Leaders whose practice **exemplifies the standard** generate innovative strategies to address complex teaching and learning challenges, as they understand and effectively use the interrelationships among shared goals, strategic actions, and resources. They gain commitment from staff and others because of the positive results they get, and they use these relationships as leverage to distribute leadership and accountability across the community in order to continuously improve outcomes beyond expectations.

When reading across a continuum, the progression is evident, with the descriptions indicating deepening knowledge, increasing task complexity, and greater collaboration with and capacity building of others. The progression of practices in the DOP reflect the following developmental intentions, with the administrator and his or her work reflecting a shift from:

Awareness	to	Implementation
Reactive	to	Proactive
Basic	to	Complex
Individual	to	Shared
Incidental	to	Strategic
Independent	to	Systemic
Compliant	to	Innovative

While each continuum represents a progression of practices, administrators' behaviors and performance are not static, so at various times their level of practice may shift back and forth across a given continuum. The effectiveness of their practice may also vary from one standard to another and from one element to another.

The conditions of specific sites vary along numerous dimensions, including, for example, the instructional capacity of the site staff or the degree of family involvement. Variations in expectations and assignments may result in different administrators needing to draw on different knowledge and skills. In recognition of such differences in context, the DOP have been carefully worded to leave room for the necessary variations in practice that are dictated by the challenges and opportunities that exist at different sites. If the context were significantly different, good practice would look different as well — while still being congruent with the standard.

Format

The DOP follow and extend the general organizational structure of the updated CPSEL — standard, element, indicators — by providing an additional level of specificity. For each CPSEL element, descriptions of leader actions are presented on a continuum that illustrates progressively more complex leadership performance. The practices include those identified in the CPSEL's example indicators, as well as other behaviors commonly expected of administrators. While the descriptions address a number of important behaviors, it is important to note that they are not exhaustive in the behaviors they cover.

The two-page DOP format is identical for each element. On the left page, the standard, element, and example indicators of practice from the CPSEL are presented, followed by a brief narrative that highlights the significance of these leader actions in guiding a school to effectively support all students to learn and thrive. On the facing page, the element is restated, and the descriptions of practice are laid out in a continuum that illustrates increasing levels of leadership skill and application. Again, these descriptions are based on the indicators of practice outlined in the CPSEL.

Terminology in This Document

Key terms used in this document were chosen in an effort to maintain a reasonable level of consistency while avoiding unnecessary repetition. The definitions and explanations provided below are intended to help clarify some of the common terms.

Administrator, leader. The standards and the DOP are intended for individuals serving in formal administrative positions in a variety of sites. The terms *administrator* and *leader* have been used to identify this role. However, in the descriptions of the continuum of practice, the term *administrator* is used for the first two levels of practice, while the term *leader* is reserved for the two highest levels — practice that meets or exemplifies the standard. This is a deliberate choice intended to highlight the shift that occurs as administrators improve their practice, moving from tactical managers to strategic instructional leaders whose efforts result in improved student learning.

Parents, families, community, stakeholders. The terms *parents* and *families* are used somewhat interchangeably in recognition of the fact that many children do not have a parent who is active in their life and, instead, are taken care of by a relative or other guardian. In this document, *community* usually refers to the larger environment of individuals and groups (e.g., businesses, associations, organizations) within a site's attendance area or beyond. *Stakeholders* refers to any person or organization with a vested interest in the site and its students. Stakeholders include school staff; families; the community (as described above); students; school, district, county office, regional, and state education agency staff; and local or state officials.

Site. The term *site* is used to acknowledge administrators working at all levels of the education system.

Staff. The term *staff* is intended to be inclusive, referring to all certificated and classified people employed at the site. Use of these terms is not intended to preclude readers from considering a broader interpretation that would include all employees (and perhaps even volunteers) at the site.

From Theory to Practice

To be successful, today's school administrators must assume multiple roles, from catalyst to manager, from expert to facilitator. Above all, they must serve as instructional leaders, their every action and decision focused on the singular goal of ensuring that all students achieve high academic standards. Beyond such broad generalizations, however, for those who aspire to leadership and those who seek to develop and nurture it, the essential question is this: What does effective leadership look like, not just in theory, but in action?

Building from the CPSEL, the DOP articulate a consensus about the knowledge, skills, and dispositions requisite to successful school leadership by laying out a set of ideas for individuals and professional communities to examine and reflect upon as they consider effective leadership practice and strategies that support all students to learn and thrive. The vision of education leadership embodied in these DOP is one in which all efforts focus on attaining education success for every student. In this vision, education achievement and equity is the goal toward which leaders guide teachers and other staff; students, parents, and guardians; and the school's broader community.

Education leaders facilitate the development and implementation of a shared vision of learning and growth of all students.

Student-Centered Vision

Leaders shape a collective vision that uses multiple measures of data and focuses on equitable access, opportunities, and outcomes for all students.

Leaders amplify the vision that every student will graduate ready for advanced learning and productive careers. They do this by collaborating with staff, students, and other stakeholders to identify the unique strengths and needs of students, paying close attention to the academic, linguistic, cultural, social-emotional, behavioral, and physical development of each learner. Leaders partner with stakeholders in examining multiple sources of information to learn about student academic progress and overall well-being. Together, they use what they learn from the data to enact their vision — creating varied learning options, addressing disparities in achievement and opportunity among student groups, and attending to students with cultural, racial, and linguistic differences, disadvantaged socio-economic backgrounds, and/or special needs.

EXAMPLE INDICATORS OF PRACTICE

1A-1 Advance support for the academic, linguistic, cultural, social-emotional, behavioral, and physical development of each learner.

1A-2 Cultivate multiple learning opportunities and support systems that build on student assets and address student needs.

1A-3 Address achievement and opportunity disparities between student groups, with attention to those with special needs; cultural, racial, and linguistic differences; and disadvantaged socio-economic backgrounds.

1A-4 Emphasize the expectation that all students will meet content and performance standards.

ELEMENT 1A / Student-Centered Vision

Leaders shape a collective vision that uses multiple measures of data and focuses on equitable access, opportunities, and outcomes for all students.

Practice that is directed toward the standard	Practice that approaches the standard	Practice that meets the standard	Practice that exemplifies the standard
The administrator understands that the site's purpose centers on increasing each student's learning and well-being. The administrator makes public and transparent her/his core belief that the site's vision encompasses the value of education and equitable opportunity. S/he uses available data to identify current opportunities and outcomes for students with various academic, linguistic, cultural, social-emotional, behavioral, and physical development needs. S/he initiates staff discussions that identify various learning opportunities and supports that build on student assets and address student needs.	The administrator communicates that the vision of all students meeting content and performance standards is central to developing and implementing instructional activities and support services. S/he works with staff to commit to a vision focused on student-centered learning and on the well-being of each student. S/he draws attention to existing equity gaps for diverse student populations. The administrator provides information for staff to learn about the range of academic, linguistic, cultural, social-emotional, behavioral, and physical development needs of the site's students. S/he builds staff capacity for implementing strategic initiatives that both build on students' assets and address their needs as a means to attain equity by closing opportunity and achievement gaps.	The leader and staff consistently work toward eliminating disparities among student groups. Working with staff, students, and others, the leader shapes a collective vision of equitable access and opportunity in support of all students' learning and well-being. S/he facilitates a review of varied sources of information about the academic, linguistic, cultural, social-emotional, behavioral, and physical development of each learner to gauge the learner's progress in meeting content and performance outcomes. The leader solicits input about ways to institutionalize equitable access and opportunities for all students to meet expected outcomes. S/he empowers staff to use their experience and expertise to cultivate multiple learning and support opportunities that align with students' diverse assets and needs.	The leader manifests the vision of all students graduating ready for college and career. S/he does so by proactively engaging staff, students, and the broader community in evidence-rich conversations about equitable opportunities and outcomes for all students' learning and well-being. S/he makes certain that these opportunities are available to, and support, students with academic, linguistic, cultural, social-emotional, behavioral, and physical development needs. In collaboration with stakeholders, s/he creatively designs and implements multiple learning opportunities with the goal of eliminating disparities in opportunity and achievement among student groups. The leader sustains effective systems for students with differing abilities, seeing to it that their needs are met with a sense of urgency and high expectations.

> **Education leaders facilitate the development and implementation of a shared vision of learning and growth of all students.**

Developing Shared Vision

Leaders engage others in a collaborative process to develop a vision of teaching and learning that is shared and supported by all stakeholders.

Leaders actualize an authentic, equitable, and action-oriented vision by engaging the full range of stakeholders. They are especially careful to include representatives of students most affected by inequitable learning opportunities and outcomes. Leaders facilitate a variety of ways for these individuals and groups to voice their values, beliefs, and aspirations for students and the site, thus generating shared leadership and accountability for vision-driven action. Leaders work with the school community to incorporate their multiple perspectives into a shared vision of learning and achievement for all students — a vision that the entire school community can understand, support, and implement consistently.

EXAMPLE INDICATORS OF PRACTICE

1B-1 Embrace diverse perspectives and craft consensus about the vision and goals.

1B-2 Communicate the vision so that the staff and school community understand it and use it for decision-making.

1B-3 Build shared accountability to achieve the vision by distributing leadership roles and responsibilities among staff and community.

1B-4 Align the vision and goals with local, state, and federal education laws and regulations.

ELEMENT 1B / Developing Shared Vision

Leaders engage others in a collaborative process to develop a vision of teaching and learning that is shared and supported by all stakeholders.

Practice that is directed toward the standard	Practice that approaches the standard	Practice that meets the standard	Practice that exemplifies the standard
The administrator invites staff and a group of community leaders to become involved in developing the site's vision. S/he introduces these individuals to relevant local, state, and federal education laws and regulations that must serve as parameters for the vision. To make stakeholders aware of the resulting vision, the administrator articulates it through a variety of communication modes. S/he asks staff for ideas about how they can use the shared vision in their work and how best to convey the vision to families.	The administrator enlists staff and other stakeholders to participate in the vision-development process. In that process, s/he presents relevant local, state, and federal laws and regulations as a guide for framing a vision of equity and fairness. Engaging with individual and groups of stakeholders, s/he facilitates the sharing of different views and helps participants reach consensus around a vision they can support. S/he asks staff involved in vision development to report to other staff about the process as it is underway and to share the vision with families, to help garner commitment to using the vision for decision-making. S/he aligns the site's vision and goals with district, state and federal regulations and links them to the student needs targeted by stakeholders.	The leader recruits a broad range of staff, students, families, and others to actively engage in an inclusive and broadly supported vision-development process. Before finalizing the vision, s/he works with others to check alignment with local, state, and federal laws and regulations. Once the vision is developed, the leader uses staff meetings and regular communications to consistently reinforce the shared vision and discuss what needs to be done to accomplish it. The leader engages staff and community leaders in taking responsibility to communicate the vision. S/he uses existing structures and systems to embed the vision in decision-making processes.	The leader mobilizes a broad range of stakeholders, offering a variety of activities to maximize their engagement in developing an authentic site vision. S/he helps staff and the community to understand local, state, and federal education laws and regulations that affect the vision, and s/he reviews and adjusts the vision as needed to create systemic coherence. S/he uses various settings to communicate the vision to all stakeholders, building broad ownership. S/he demonstrates the vision's relevance for day-to-day work by holding staff accountable for making progress on strategies that are included in the vision. S/he models accountability by referencing it in progress reports at community meetings and events and asking other school community leaders to do the same.

Education leaders facilitate the development and implementation of a shared vision of learning and growth of all students.

Vision Planning and Implementation

Leaders guide and monitor decisions, actions, and outcomes using the shared vision and goals.

Leaders recognize that a well-articulated vision serves as both a driver and the touchstone for all courses of action and decisions. They advance the vision by supporting others to understand and use the site's vision-driven goals to guide the learning and growth of all students. Leaders establish structures and processes to periodically revisit the vision and to review evidence of student learning and program results. They use this evidence to adjust goals and activities to better align with the vision, working with staff and the community to continuously clarify and improve the actions needed to reach the vision. Leaders are then able to monitor and equitably allocate human, fiscal, and technological resources in support of the vision.

EXAMPLE INDICATORS OF PRACTICE

1C-1   Include all stakeholders in a process of continuous improvement (reflection, revision, and modification) based on the systematic review of evidence and progress.

1C-2   Use evidence (including, but not limited to, student achievement, attendance, behavior and school-climate data, research, and best practices) to shape and revise plans, programs, and activities that advance the vision.

1C-3   Marshal, equitably allocate, and efficiently use human, fiscal, and technological resources aligned with the vision of learning for all students.

Leaders guide and monitor decisions, actions, and outcomes using the shared vision and goals.

Practice that is directed toward the standard	Practice that approaches the standard	Practice that meets the standard	Practice that exemplifies the standard
The administrator recognizes that, to realize the vision, s/he must direct planning and implementation activities. S/he understands that plans may evolve as circumstances change so implementation plans for the site's vision should be reviewed and updated if needed. S/he identifies multiple sources of evidence to be collected to determine whether the implementation plan is helping the site address its vision. The administrator refers to the site's vision when allocating resources.	The administrator guides development of an action plan detailing specific goals and strategies directed toward achieving the vision. S/he informally checks the effectiveness of selected strategies at regular staff meetings and checks overall progress more formally during annual program reviews that include additional stakeholders. The administrator works with staff to adjust activities in the action plan, as needed, in order to continuously progress toward the site's vision and goals. The administrator uses the site's vision and goals as the basis for prioritizing and aligning available human, fiscal, and technological resources.	The leader engages staff and stakeholders in a process of ongoing monitoring and assessment of progress toward realizing the vision. S/he works with staff to systematically collect and analyze data about the site's growth and gaps. The leader expects staff to communicate all results to site families and community members. S/he uses the results to build interest in and commitment to updating the implementation plans that are necessary to achieve equitable results. The leader monitors the alignment of effort and resources to properly support the plan for implementing the vision and goals. To that end, s/he maximizes existing resources and identifies any additional human, fiscal, or technological resources that are needed.	The leader works with staff and stakeholders to sustain a system of continuous improvement based on ongoing review and analysis of evidence to determine results and potential modification of activities. The leader presents stakeholders with varied opportunities to provide feedback on the effectiveness of implementation plans, and s/he advocates for careful consideration of stakeholder input. Using a variety of evidence, the leader reprioritizes existing human, fiscal, and technological resources and seeks new and creatively conceived resources, as needed.

Education leaders shape a collaborative culture of teaching and learning, informed by professional standards and focused on student and professional growth.

ELEMENT 2A

Professional Learning Culture

Leaders promote a culture in which staff engage in individual and collective professional learning that results in their continuous improvement and high performance.

Leaders cultivate a rich learning environment for students and staff alike. They shape a professional culture that affirms staff members' shared responsibility for continuous learning. Leaders guide and support teachers in their professional responsibilities, in individual development, and in their shared growth as a staff, ensuring that professional learning is embedded in their work and is based on research. Leaders recognize that a site's staff, like its student population, represents a range of experiences, skills, and learning styles, and develop a supportive environment for adult learning accordingly.

EXAMPLE INDICATORS OF PRACTICE

2A-1 Establish coherent, research-based professional learning aligned with organizational vision and goals for educator and student growth.

2A-2 Promote professional learning plans that focus on real situations and specific needs related to increasing the learning and well-being of all staff and students.

2A-3 Capitalize on the diverse experiences and abilities of staff to plan, implement, and assess professional learning.

2A-4 Strengthen staff trust, shared responsibility, and leadership by instituting structures and processes that promote collaborative inquiry and problem solving.

ELEMENT 2A / **Professional Learning Culture**

Leaders promote a culture in which staff engage in individual and collective professional learning that results in their continuous improvement and high performance.

Practice that is directed toward the standard	Practice that approaches the standard	Practice that meets the standard	Practice that exemplifies the standard
The administrator recognizes that professional growth is essential for overall progress toward student achievement. S/he is knowledgeable about the state standards for educators and for professional learning. S/he presents staff with expectations that they will develop individual learning plans linking their growth with the site's vision and goals. The administrator solicits staff to participate in planning professional learning activities that reflect staff perspectives. S/he is beginning to use structures and processes to promote collaboration and joint problem solving.	The administrator seeks staff input in order to provide a range of professional learning for individuals and groups of staff that reflects the site's shared vision. S/he guides development and use of site and individual professional learning plans to identify goals, strategies, and activities to increase the knowledge and skills necessary to meet student needs. The administrator reviews the individual plans to identify staff strengths in research-based and best practices, and s/he encourages staff to share their expertise in planning and delivering professional learning activities for the site. S/he creates opportunities for staff to try out learning structures and processes, such as collaborative inquiry and joint problem solving, and then to share results with the rest of the staff.	The leader collaborates with staff in designing and implementing coherent professional learning opportunities that are aligned to the site's vision, and s/he consistently applies research-based practices tied to teaching and student growth outcomes. S/he makes sure that professional growth activities for staff are embedded in relevant work; address the range of staff experience, skills, and needs; and are documented in professional learning plans for individuals and for the full staff. The leader leverages staff expertise by providing regular opportunities for them to serve as leaders in planning, convening, and assessing professional learning activities. S/he builds staff trust and confidence by implementing structures and processes that promote collaborative inquiry and problem solving.	The leader uses her/his deep understanding of research and best practices for standards-based teaching and learning to collaboratively organize and guide a coherent system of professional learning. S/he oversees a system that targets and extends the site's vision for student and staff growth. S/he shares leadership with staff in building and implementing individual and site-wide professional learning plans that document a strategic and systematic approach to continuously improving instruction, support, and student growth. S/he co-leads development, implementation, and assessment of new professional learning structures and processes that integrate staff assets and needs with inquiry and problem-solving practices related to meeting site goals.

Education leaders shape a collaborative culture of teaching and learning, informed by professional standards and focused on student and professional growth.

ELEMENT 2B

Curriculum and Instruction

Leaders guide and support the implementation of standards-based curriculum, instruction, and assessments that address student expectations and outcomes.

Leaders drive adjustments in the instructional program, aimed at eliminating opportunity and achievement gaps. They leverage their deep understanding of teaching and learning to implement a coherent and continuously improving instructional system. Together with staff, they engage in regular inquiry and assessments about the effectiveness of their program in meeting the diverse needs, and building from the diverse assets, of all students. By involving all staff in a process of continuous monitoring and refinement, leaders help individual staff to calibrate their practice and gauge the effectiveness of their instructional strategies in serving all students equitably.

EXAMPLE INDICATORS OF PRACTICE

2B-1 Develop a shared understanding of adopted standards-based curriculum that reflects student content and performance expectations.

2B-2 Promote and monitor the use of state frameworks and guides that offer evidence-based instructional and support strategies to increase learning for diverse student assets and needs.

2B-3 Provide access to a variety of resources that are needed for the effective instruction and differentiated support of all students.

2B-4 Guide and monitor the alignment of curriculum, instruction, assessment, and professional practice.

Leaders guide and support the implementation of standards-based curriculum, instruction, and assessments that address student expectations and outcomes.

Practice that is directed toward the standard	Practice that approaches the standard	Practice that meets the standard	Practice that exemplifies the standard
The administrator references student content and performance expectations in discussions with staff about curriculum and instruction. S/he has a broad understanding of content and performance standards on which the adopted curriculum is based. The administrator gathers information about resources needed for delivering state-adopted curriculum.	The administrator guides staff in developing a shared understanding of curriculum, instructional strategies, and state assessments that is shaped by student content and performance standards. S/he monitors whether staff who are working in content areas that have state frameworks and guides are using them when planning lessons. The administrator seeks staff input to understand whether staff have adequate resources to support the site's diverse students in meeting standards.	The leader creates subject- and grade-level teams that draw on a shared understanding of student content and performance standards to plan goals and instruction. S/he works with staff to align curriculum with state expectations for all students and to use evidence-based instructional and support strategies. S/he engages staff in determining the varied resources needed for effective instruction and support services for students with a wide range of assets and needs. As part of sharing responsibility, the leader guides and facilitates staff involvement in assessing and continuously improving the alignment of curriculum, instruction, assessment, and professional learning.	The leader engages staff, students, and other stakeholders in developing a deep understanding of student content and performance expectations in order to solicit their participation in designing and providing innovative learning opportunities. S/he works with the established instructional leadership team to design effective curriculum for students with diverse assets and needs and to implement evidence-based instructional and support strategies. S/he shares leadership with staff in identifying, acquiring, and distributing a variety of resources that are relevant in supporting all students to graduate ready for college and career. The leader also works with staff and other stakeholders in gauging the success of implementing a seamless system of curriculum, instruction, assessment, and professional learning.

> Education leaders shape a collaborative culture of teaching and learning, informed by professional standards and focused on student and professional growth.

ELEMENT 2C

Assessment and Accountability

Leaders develop and use assessment and accountability systems to monitor, improve, and extend educator practice, program outcomes, and student learning.

Leaders mobilize staff and community members to organize and sustain a rigorous and useful accountability system that guides teaching and learning. They align their accountability system with state and district academic standards, accountability tools, and assessments, while also supporting the development and use of internal accountability strategies aimed at building the organization's capacity to achieve its goals. Leaders work with staff individually and collectively to clarify desired student outcomes and identify multiple strategies by which students' progress toward these goals can be determined. To do this, leaders facilitate staff engagement in regular reviews of evidence of student learning to consistently plan and adjust both instruction and professional learning.

EXAMPLE INDICATORS OF PRACTICE

2C-1   Define clear purposes, goals, and working agreements for collecting and sharing information about professional practice and student outcomes.

2C-2   Guide staff and the community in regular disaggregation and analysis of local and state student assessment results and program data.

2C-3   Use information from a variety of sources to guide program and professional learning planning, implementation, and revisions.

2C-4   Use professional expectations and standards to guide, monitor, support, and supervise to improve teaching and learning.

2C-5   Apply a variety of tools and technology to gather feedback, organize and analyze multiple data sources, and monitor student progress directed toward improving teaching and learning.

ELEMENT 2C / Assessment and Accountability

Leaders develop and use assessment and accountability systems to monitor, improve, and extend educator practice, program outcomes, and student learning.

Practice that is directed toward the standard	Practice that approaches the standard	Practice that meets the standard	Practice that exemplifies the standard
The administrator understands various purposes and measures for collecting and using information about program, professional-practice, and student outcomes. S/he understands how to analyze state's student-assessment and program information and how it must be protected. S/he summarizes data and presents it to staff, initiating staff discussions about using information from a variety of sources to fairly assess program, personnel, or student results. S/he is developing knowledge about technology for gathering feedback, organizing data sources, and monitoring student progress. S/he uses teaching standards as the foundation for collecting data on the professional practice of staff.	The administrator works with staff to clarify their understanding of, and commitment to, collecting and using state and local information to assess program effectiveness, professional practice, and student outcomes. S/he reviews and shares disaggregated student and program data with staff and provides training on using multiple measures and varied sources of data to draw fair and accurate conclusions. The administrator works with a team to pilot and recommend to staff various technologies to use when gathering and monitoring site-generated information. The administrator explains district expectations for how s/he and the staff will use professional standards to guide, support, monitor, and assess efforts to improve professional practice.	The leader works with all staff members to define clear goals and working agreements related to measuring and using outcome data for program, professional-practice, and student accountability. The leader facilitates and supports staff in using formative and interim site and student assessments to gauge short- and long-term progress in meeting expected student standards. In regularly scheduled sessions, the leader and staff extend their collective capacity to apply a variety of tools and technology, disaggregate and analyze local and state assessment results, and identify changes needed to improve the site's program and staff practices. The leader collaborates with staff in using professional standards as the basis for staff professional learning and the supervision process.	The leader engages the staff, students, and community in discussing assessment and accountability measures that inform progress on program, professional-practice, and student outcomes. S/he facilitates regular opportunities for staff and community to monitor, disaggregate, and analyze local and state student assessment and program results, to build transparent accountability. With community support, s/he and staff employ resources that enable broad and deep data collection needed for fair and accurate conclusions about professional and student performance. S/he applies that data in driving changes needed to continuously strengthen teaching and learning. S/he shares leadership for incorporating professional standards into reviewing, supporting, and supervising all professional practice.

STANDARD 2 Instructional Leadership / **17**

Education leaders manage the organization to cultivate a safe and productive learning and working environment.

ELEMENT 3A

Operations and Facilities

Leaders provide and oversee a functional, safe, and clean learning environment.

Leaders foster an environment in which safety and accessibility are fundamental elements of student learning and well-being. They orchestrate a complex network of site and district staff, along with community members, local authorities, specialists, and other stakeholders, to prepare for and execute effective responses to current and anticipated emergencies and challenges. Leaders sustain a communitywide focus on day-to-day and long-term operations, facilities, and health and welfare services that attend to the differentiated needs of students and staff. They also facilitate the acquisition and disbursement of equipment, materials, and technology that target students' and staff's academic, linguistic, cultural, social-emotional, and physical requirements so that all students can fully participate in learning.

EXAMPLE INDICATORS OF PRACTICE

3A-1 Systematically review the physical plant and grounds to ensure that they are safe, meet Americans with Disabilities Act (ADA) requirements, and comply with conditions that support accessibility for all students.

3A-2 Collaborate with the district to monitor and maintain student services (e.g., food, transportation) that contribute to student learning, health, and welfare.

3A-3 Manage the acquisition, distribution, and maintenance of equipment, materials, and technology needed to meet the academic, linguistic, cultural, social-emotional, and physical requirements of students.

3A-4 Work with stakeholders and experts to plan and implement emergency and risk management procedures for individuals and the site.

Leaders provide and oversee a functional, safe, and clean learning environment.

Practice that is directed toward the standard	Practice that approaches the standard	Practice that meets the standard	Practice that exemplifies the standard
The administrator understands and commits to operating a well-functioning, clean, and safe site that supports an environment focused on student learning. S/he knows about the state and local mandates for meeting accessibility, health, and welfare requirements and has a written emergency plan. The administrator provides staff and students with materials, equipment, and technology necessary for operations and instruction, keeping students with special needs in mind. S/he shares student services, operations and maintenance procedures with staff and follows safety and security regulations established by the district.	The administrator develops a schedule for regularly inspecting the site for any problems that might compromise a safe, well-functioning learning environment. S/he schedules safety and security drills. S/he enlists site and district staff for a committee to help identify accessibility, safety, health, and welfare issues to be considered for inclusion in their federal, state, and local improvement goals and plans. The administrator establishes a process for purchasing and monitoring materials, equipment, and technology for operations and instruction, and s/he encourages general education staff to work with staff specialists to address student needs for additional learning support.	The leader collaborates with staff in promoting effective operations, accessibility, safety, health, and welfare policies and practices. S/he directs the acquisition, distribution, and maintenance of equipment, materials, and technology for all staff and students, with attention to the academic, linguistic, cultural, social-emotional, and physical needs of students. The leader convenes, facilitates, and collaborates with district staff, stakeholders and experts to plan, implement, and communicate emergency and risk management procedures for individuals and the site. S/he sees that students and staff are trained in, and regularly practice, emergency and risk management procedures. S/he works with all staff, the district, and other partners to coordinate and sustain student services that support student learning, safety, health, and welfare.	The leader shares leadership with staff and others in overseeing a coherent, integrated operations system. S/he and staff engage students, families, and the community as partners in maintaining buildings and grounds and keeping equipment and technology in good condition. The leader advocates for acquiring and distributing equipment, materials, and technology that supports all staff and students, including students with specific academic, linguistic, cultural, social-emotional, and physical needs. S/he works with the staff, district, local authorities, and other specialists to anticipate accessibility, health, welfare, and safety challenges and has contingency plans and cooperative agreements in place to address them quickly.

Education leaders manage the organization to cultivate a safe and productive learning and working environment.

Plans and Procedures

Leaders establish structures and employ policies and processes that support students to graduate ready for college and career.

Leaders purposefully engineer the infrastructure of the site to operate in support of the core work of teaching and learning. They organize, assign, and schedule staff and students in ways that maximize staff collaboration and student learning. Leaders establish and manage legal and working agreements that set clear expectations and result in a secure, supportive, and collaborative environment for all students, staff, and community members. Leaders include stakeholders in problem-solving and decision-making processes to establish policies, procedures, and structures and to advise on operational decisions that are consistently focused on equitable outcomes for all students.

EXAMPLE INDICATORS OF PRACTICE

3B-1 Develop schedules and assign placements that are student-centered and maximize instructional time and staff collaboration.

3B-2 Manage legal and contractual agreements and storage of confidential records (both paper and electronic) to ensure student security and confidentiality.

3B-3 Set clear working agreements that support sharing problems, practices, and results within a safe and supportive environment.

3B-4 Engage stakeholders in using problem-solving and decision-making processes and distributed leadership to develop, monitor, evaluate, and revise plans and programs.

Leaders establish structures and employ policies and processes that support students to graduate ready for college and career.

Practice that is directed toward the standard	Practice that approaches the standard	Practice that meets the standard	Practice that exemplifies the standard
The administrator considers site goals and the need to protect instructional time as key factors in developing plans and procedures. S/he follows and directs established practices for determining student and staff placements, assignments, and schedules. S/he understands and applies laws and district requirements to the maintenance of staff and student confidentiality. The administrator sets up clear communication processes to share expectations and procedures with staff in a timely fashion. S/he understands the importance of staff involvement in solving problems and sharing practices, and s/he encourages staff to participate in discussions that the administrator structures.	The administrator guides staff in making student placements and scheduling decisions that are focused first on student learning. The administrator assigns staff responsibilities with attention to protecting instructional time, and s/he sets expectations, agendas, and meeting time for staff to share problems, practices, and results with others. S/he establishes and maintains open lines of communication with staff for timely information flow, providing staff with information that builds their understanding of issues related to legal and contractual agreements and to student and staff security and privacy. When necessary, s/he organizes ad hoc committees for staff to identify potential changes aimed to improve site processes or procedures or to monitor and revise plans and programs.	The leader works with staff to develop processes and structures for organizing students and staff to consistently focus on instruction and student outcomes. S/he models and encourages open, safe communications, providing staff with opportunities to share in problem solving and decision-making, while safeguarding student and staff confidentiality. S/he shares leadership for moving policies into operational decisions related to curriculum planning, instruction, support programs, and assessments. The leader manages legal and contractual agreements, gathering staff and other stakeholder input about the agreements' impact on teaching and learning. The leader protects time for staff to collaborate on instruction, assessments, and procedures affecting instruction. S/he engages staff and other stakeholders in reviewing the impact of established policies and processes on all students and in revising short- and long-term plans as necessary.	The leader, staff, and other stakeholders capitalize on their collective policy, procedures, and working agreements to organize and structure student-centered learning and support options. The leader reinforces and protects open, safe communications so that staff take multiple opportunities to share leadership on instructional and management issues. S/he cultivates shared responsibility and accountability among staff and other stakeholders to guarantee confidentiality and safeguard the privacy of staff, students, parents, and other community members. The leader facilitates opportunities for staff to lead short- and long-term cycles of planning with stakeholders, reviewing and applying relevant data and technology to determine the status of shared goals and outcomes.

Education leaders manage the organization to cultivate a safe and productive learning and working environment.

ELEMENT 3C

Climate

Leaders facilitate safe, fair, and respectful environments that meet the intellectual, linguistic, cultural, social-emotional, and physical needs of each learner.

Leaders cultivate an environment in which all students and staff experience a sense of belonging and feel valued, so that everyone can engage in individual and collective learning. They promote dialogue, accountability, and a sense of community that come together to support and focus on a positive physical and emotional learning culture for all students. Rather than over-relying on punitive strategies like suspension or expulsion, leaders work with students, staff, and other stakeholders to specify, implement, and monitor a positive and equitable student responsibility-and-behavior system. Leaders build and nurture a safe, fair, and respectful school climate in which everyone involved learns and practices self-discipline, empathy, and accountability.

EXAMPLE INDICATORS
OF PRACTICE

3C-1 Strengthen school climate through participation, engagement, connection, and a sense of belonging among all students and staff.

3C-2 Implement a positive and equitable student responsibility and behavior system with teaching, intervention and prevention strategies and protocols that are clear, fair, incremental, restorative, culturally responsive, and celebrate student and school achievement.

3C-3 Consistently monitor, review, and respond to attendance, disciplinary, and other relevant data to improve school climate and student engagement and ensure that management practices are free from bias and equitably applied to all students.

Leaders facilitate safe, fair, and respectful environments that meet the intellectual, linguistic, cultural, social-emotional, and physical needs of each learner.

Practice that is directed toward the standard	Practice that approaches the standard	Practice that meets the standard	Practice that exemplifies the standard
The administrator draws staff attention to the importance of a safe, positive site climate for student success. S/he encourages staff participation in developing respectful environments that address varied staff and student needs. The administrator establishes and reinforces a student behavior system that includes the teaching of rules and consequences for any actions that hinder teaching and learning. S/he conveys clear behavioral expectations that are equally applicable to all students and encourages staff to acknowledge student achievements and behaviors that meet expectations. The administrator collects data about individual and group attendance and discipline referrals, communicating results to staff so they can use the data to help improve school climate.	The administrator builds staff and student capacity to understand and value the role of physical and emotional safety at the site in enabling student learning and well-being. S/he convenes staff to learn about behavior-management systems that stress fair and incremental responses to student discipline issues and that incorporate culturally responsive strategies. With staff, s/he discusses and uses site-specific data to raise questions about any student groups that are consistently identified for disciplinary action and the possible individual and collective reasons for any imbalances. The administrator engages a committee of staff and other stakeholders in developing or updating a site behavior-management plan that addresses student attendance, participation, discipline, and achievement. Together, committee members commit to working on improvement goals and acknowledging accomplishments.	The leader enlists the assistance of staff, students, and other stakeholders in establishing and monitoring an environment that employs engagement and participation strategies to increase a sense of belonging, self-worth, and dignity among all staff and students. S/he works with staff and students to implement and oversee a behavior-management system with incremental interventions based on prevention, personal responsibility, and restorative practices. S/he leads and collaborates with staff and stakeholders in analyzing and responding to all relevant data to build and sustain a safe, fair, and respectful climate that meets the intellectual, linguistic, cultural, social-emotional, and physical needs of each learner. S/he initiates regular celebrations to mark student, staff, and site accomplishments.	The leader cultivates shared leadership among staff, students, and other stakeholders, empowering them to use disaggregated data to identify factors that impact student engagement, connection, and sense of belonging. S/he facilitates an integrated instructional and behavior-management system in which staff and other stakeholders lead and implement culturally responsive strategies that engage students and staff in individual and collective learning. The leader consistently sponsors actions that promote a safe, fair, and respectful environment for all students, with extra support for students with intellectual, linguistic, cultural, social-emotional, physical, or other needs. In collaboration with others, the leader regularly reviews progress and next steps for continuously improving site climate and regularly acknowledges individual and group accomplishments.

Education leaders manage the organization to cultivate a safe and productive learning and working environment.

ELEMENT 3D

Fiscal and Human Resources

Leaders align fiscal and human resources and manage policies and contractual agreements that build a productive learning environment.

Leaders mobilize and maximize resources for the program, then allocate the resources to secure equitable outcomes for all students. They understand that achieving equitable results is not based on students receiving identical resources, but, rather, is based on students receiving the specific resources that they need in order to graduate ready for college and career. Leaders have a thorough understanding of student and site needs and use it as a foundation for making transparent decisions about a wide range of resources — not just regular and special funding, but also personnel, the physical plant, instructional materials, and time. Because effective staff are a key determinant of student learning, leaders hone in on personnel hiring, placement, professional learning, and performance assessment practices that result in productive and supportive teaching and learning.

EXAMPLE INDICATORS OF PRACTICE

3D-1 Provide a clear rationale for decisions and distribute resources equitably to advance a shared vision and goals focused on the needs of all students.

3D-2 Work with the district and school community to focus on both short- and long-term fiscal management.

3D-3 Actively direct staff hiring and placement to match staff capacity with student academic and support goals.

3D-4 Engage staff in professional learning and formative assessments with specific feedback for continuous growth.

3D-5 Conduct personnel evaluations to improve teaching and learning, in keeping with district and state policies.

3D-6 Establish and monitor expectations for staff behavior and performance, recognizing positive results and responding to poor performance and/or inappropriate or illegal behavior directly and in a timely and systematic manner.

ELEMENT 3D / Fiscal and Human Resources

Leaders align fiscal and human resources and manage policies and contractual agreements that build a productive learning environment.

Practice that is directed toward the standard	Practice that approaches the standard	Practice that meets the standard	Practice that exemplifies the standard
The administrator understands federal, state, and local requirements and policies for managing fiscal and human resources. S/he references these requirements when talking with staff about fair short- and long-term resource decisions for local funding and accountability plans. The administrator knows the importance of professional learning for improving staff and student outcomes, and s/he solicits staff input on varied options before making plans final. S/he follows district human resource policies and labor agreements for establishing staff expectations, providing professional learning, monitoring performance, and conducting evaluations. S/he provides timely feedback to individual staff members, acknowledging positive accomplishments, and responds to poor or inappropriate behavior.	The administrator directs financial and personnel resources toward activities included in the site's vision, goals, and plans. S/he builds staff and community understanding of federal, state, and local regulations regarding fiscal allocations, uses, and restrictions. S/he initiates opportunities for inclusive, transparent, and sound short- and long-term fiscal and human resource planning and monitoring for local funding and accountability plans. S/he works with staff groups to coordinate contractual agreements and the equitable distribution of fiscal and human resources with student-centered interests and needs. S/he engages staff in a range of learning opportunities, from increasing individual knowledge to advising the administrator on hiring, placement, professional learning, and evaluation matters. S/he offers individual staff feedback on growth and performance during the evaluation process. S/he recognizes staff achievements and quickly attends to any poor or inappropriate staff behavior.	The leader engages staff and stakeholders in aligning fiscal and human resources to the site's vision and plans for a productive learning environment. S/he helps stakeholders use short- and long-term management strategies and procedures that reinforce consensus on consistent and equitable distribution of fiscal and human resources. The leader is deliberate in putting student academic and support goals at the center of staff hiring, placement, and professional learning decisions, working within established policies and contractual agreements. S/he promotes the continuous improvement of all staff by supporting a system of professional learning and personnel evaluation. With each staff member, the leader collects and uses varied evidence to evaluate individual professional growth and performance in meeting student outcome goals. S/he consistently monitors staff behavior and performance and provides specific and actionable feedback that addresses problems directly and swiftly.	The leader partners with staff and other stakeholders, through collaborative agreements and processes, to monitor, leverage and equitably align all fiscal and human resources with the site's goals, including a productive learning environment and desired student outcomes. The leader bases staff hiring, placement, professional learning, and evaluation on assets and gaps in the staff's and site's capacity to equitably and effectively serve all students. Together, the leader and staff create a coherent system of professional learning and support for continuous improvement that integrates contractual agreements and established policies. For individual performance evaluations, the leader emphasizes a collaborative process that uses systematic feedback and multiple forms of evidence to assess areas of strength and needed improvement. The leader immediately remedies poor performance or inappropriate behavior.

Education leaders collaborate with families and other stakeholders to address diverse student and community interests and mobilize community resources.

ELEMENT 4A

Parent and Family Engagement

Leaders meaningfully involve all parents and families, including under-represented communities, in student learning and support programs.

Leaders act upon their belief that engaging and respecting families is valuable in community-building. They model regular in-person and written interactions with students' families in a manner that encourages supporting the meaningful participation of families, both in important school matters and in supporting their children's learning. Leaders utilize a range of knowledge, skills, and capacities to bring forth the perspectives of the community and use them to inform the work of the site. They specifically involve families from underrepresented populations in proportion to the diversity of the community. They capitalize on the linguistic, cultural, and economic diversity of their community in order to enrich and strengthen relationships between the site and students' families.

EXAMPLE INDICATORS OF PRACTICE

4A-1 Establish a welcoming environment for family participation and education by recognizing and respecting diverse family goals and aspirations for students.

4A-2 Follow guidelines for communication and participation established in federal and state mandates, district policies, and legal agreements.

4A-3 Solicit input from and communicate regularly with all parents and families in ways that are accessible and understandable.

4A-4 Engage families with staff to establish academic programs and supports that address individual and collective student assets and needs.

4A-5 Facilitate a reciprocal relationship with families that encourages them to assist the school and to participate in opportunities that extend their capacity to support students.

Parent and Family Engagement

Leaders meaningfully involve all parents and families, including underrepresented communities, in student learning and support programs.

Practice that is directed toward the standard	Practice that approaches the standard	Practice that meets the standard	Practice that exemplifies the standard
The administrator is aware that parents and families have varied goals for students. S/he is aware of research and regulations regarding family involvement in site activities. S/he guides staff in identifying and prioritizing needs related to meaningful family engagement in student academic programs and expresses an expectation that staff will strengthen current practices. The administrator facilitates development of a plan for increased family engagement that brings in traditionally underrepresented communities, and that aims to grow staff capacity for working effectively with diverse families. S/he works with staff to strengthen communications with the range of diverse families and to invite families to participate in their children's schooling.	The administrator understands the importance of recognizing diverse parent and family goals and aspirations for students. S/he stresses that federal, state, and local regulations set expectations for families to be active players in developing their students' academic and support plans. S/he initiates a plan to invite meaningful participation by families, including those from traditionally underrepresented communities. S/he prompts staff to identify specific site activities and committees that might benefit from including a broader range of family perspectives. The administrator develops staff commitment to making parent and family participation an integral part of planning and to reviewing goals, operations, and results related to that participation. S/he works with staff to strengthen and clarify communication that delivers information to families and that describes specific opportunities and processes for their participation in meaningful site activities.	The leader creates a respectful culture that stresses the involvement of all students' parents and families, including those who add to the school community's linguistic, cultural, and economic diversity. S/he uses mandates, policies, and legal agreements to help shape staff and community expectations for families to have a strong voice in airing concerns, ideas, and interests. The leader collaborates with staff and families, including those from underrepresented communities, in finding ways to make all communications timely, accessible, and understandable. The leader, with staff, engages family members to help in decision-making about academic programs and supports that build on individual and collective student assets and address their needs. S/he solicits a variety of interactions with families to exchange information and facilitates reciprocal relations that further build site capacity to achieve desired student and site outcomes.	The leader shares responsibility with staff and families to create and sustain a climate and culture in which respect for diverse viewpoints is expected and all stakeholders empathize with others' perspectives. The leader's behavior serves as a model for enacting strong collaborative relationships with diverse families that makes them feel valued and connected to the site vision and student goals. S/he guides staff and others in consistently following federal and state requirements and legal agreements as they co-create and implement innovative communications. As part of an ongoing partnership, staff and families collaborate in determining which academic and support programs to implement. Together, they then monitor the effectiveness with which the programs are tailored for individuals, groups of students, or all students. The leader and staff form mutually beneficial relationships with families, recognizing assets and areas of growth needed for both the site and the families in order to support student learning and well-being.

STANDARD 4
Family and Community
Engagement

Education leaders collaborate with families and other stakeholders to address diverse student and community interests and mobilize community resources.

ELEMENT 4B

Community Partnerships

Leaders establish community partnerships that promote and support students to meet performance and content expectations and graduate ready for college and career.

Leaders forge strategic partnerships and networking relationships to benefit students and the site. In considering these affiliations, leaders demonstrate deep understanding of the strengths and needs of their students and their site and analyze the potential benefits of the relationship against the obligations that the partnership might incur. They are knowledgeable about seeking out and pursuing partnership opportunities at the local, regional, and broader levels. Once a partnership is established, leaders nurture fair and respectful collaborations that advance the site's vision and goals.

EXAMPLE INDICATORS OF PRACTICE

4B-1   Incorporate information about family and community expectations and needs into decision-making and activities.

4B-2   Share leadership responsibility by establishing community, business, institutional, and civic partnerships that invest in and support the vision and goals.

4B-3   Treat all stakeholder groups with fairness and respect, and work to bring consensus on key issues that affect student learning and well-being.

4B-4   Participate in local activities that engage staff and community members in communicating school successes to the broader community.

Leaders establish community partnerships that promote and support students to meet performance and content expectations and graduate ready for college and career.

Practice that is directed toward the standard	Practice that approaches the standard	Practice that meets the standard	Practice that exemplifies the standard
The administrator is knowledgeable about the need to collect information regarding community expectations to inform decision-making and provides opportunities for such input. S/he initiates partnerships with community groups to solicit funds and other resources to address site needs. The administrator invites community members into the site and initiates relationships that signal her/his interest in establishing fair and respectful partnerships to address expectations for students. S/he periodically meets with community-service and local news organizations to share site news and accomplishments.	The administrator establishes a plan to engage community members, organizations, businesses, and institutions in partnerships that can help support site goals. S/he involves staff groups in identifying potential partners and broadening the focus of partnerships to support student readiness for college and career. S/he reminds staff to consider family and community expectations for students in their own planning and decision-making processes. The administrator encourages staff to deepen their commitment to, and hone their skills for, treating all partner groups with fairness and respect. The administrator communicates with key community organizations and leaders about site needs, activities, and accomplishments.	The leader regularly collaborates with stakeholders to pursue and maintain mutually beneficial partnerships with a range of stakeholders, including business and community members, organizations and agencies, county offices of education, and universities. S/he regularly reinforces for staff and others that partnerships are directed toward reaching the site's vision of all students becoming ready for college and career. S/he models fair and respectful engagement with community members and partner organizations, incorporating their diverse perspectives when planning and assessing education programs and services. S/he is consistently visible, accessible, and responsive in interacting with a broad range of community members to promote site and student successes.	The leader shares leadership for engaging a broad range of stakeholders to communicate their expectations and needs, then using that information in program planning and decision-making directed toward the site's vision and goals. Together, s/he and staff build and sustain a variety of long-term, mutually beneficial partnerships with a range of local and national organizations. S/he is skilled in negotiating community partnerships that reflect shared goals and decisions that are widely understood and supported by stakeholders. S/he monitors and reinforces staff and community agreements to operate inclusive partnerships with fairness and respect. S/he is highly visible in local activities and proactive in regularly delivering progress reports that staff, students, and families communicate, in turn, to the broader community.

Education leaders collaborate with families and other stakeholders to address diverse student and community interests and mobilize community resources.

ELEMENT 4C

Community Resources and Services

Leaders leverage and integrate community resources and services to meet the varied needs of all students.

Leaders actively leverage community resources to most effectively serve their students. They are knowledgeable about the academic, mental health, linguistic, cultural, social-emotional, and physical needs of their students and about what resources are available in their local community to help meet these needs. Leaders work with their staff to integrate community services with site programs, making information about community resources available to families and/or working with agencies to bring specific services to the site. They ensure that when faced with situations in which students are not progressing, staff consider every available avenue and resource to support student learning.

EXAMPLE INDICATORS OF PRACTICE

4C-1 Seek out and collaborate with community programs and services that assist students who need academic, mental health, linguistic, cultural, social-emotional, physical, or other support to succeed in school.

4C-2 Build mutually beneficial relationships with external organizations to coordinate the use of school and community facilities.

4C-3 Work with community emergency and welfare agencies to develop positive relationships.

4C-4 Secure community support to sustain existing resources and add new resources that address emerging student needs.

Leaders leverage and integrate community resources and services to meet the varied needs of all students.

Practice that is directed toward the standard	Practice that approaches the standard	Practice that meets the standard	Practice that exemplifies the standard
The administrator is aware that students and their families sometimes need extra support for students to be successful in learning. S/he reviews available data to identify areas in which students would benefit from community support services. S/he researches and identifies external resources that provide academic, cognitive, linguistic, cultural, social-emotional, physical, or other supports. The administrator and staff develop an outreach plan for contacting community resource and service providers. They also explore how the site and community services can cooperate to increase resources.	The administrator works with staff to assess specific academic, cognitive, linguistic, cultural, social-emotional, physical, or other support needs of the site's students and families. S/he uses multiple sources of data to identify areas in which community resources and services provide the support her/his students need to succeed. The administrator initiates linkages between the site and community service, emergency, and welfare agencies that most directly match site needs and can offer support. S/he works with select staff to develop options for site and community coordination of services, to make the most of resources. The administrator and staff communicate with families in understandable ways about existing community services and how to access them.	The leader and staff seek out and collaborate with community services that support the academic, cognitive, linguistic, cultural, social-emotional, physical, and economic needs that inhibit student learning and well-being. The leader supports staff in expanding their capacity to respond effectively to student and family needs and to broker connections between students and families and appropriate on-site or community-based services. S/he and staff are committed to building and sustaining positive partnerships and working agreements with local community, emergency, and welfare agencies by building mutually beneficial relationships that coordinate the use of site and community facilities and services. S/he capitalizes on community relationships to sustain existing resources and identify new resources to address needs.	The leader establishes a culture in which staff and stakeholders engage every available avenue and resource to support student learning and well-being. S/he advocates for students and their families by actively eliciting support for them from varied community service agencies and by connecting students and families with those services. The leader collaborates with staff and other stakeholders to regularly assess emerging needs and to review the effectiveness of partnerships and student progress related to support services. Together, they develop and implement new programs and delivery systems based on those data. The leader continuously seeks new opportunities to develop positive relationships, and s/he partners with external organizations that have mutual interests in sustaining and extending community resources to support students in reaching their goals.

Education leaders make decisions, model, and behave in ways that demonstrate professionalism, ethics, integrity, justice, and equity and hold staff to the same standard.

ELEMENT 5A

Reflective Practice

Leaders act upon a personal code of ethics that requires continuous reflection and learning.

Leaders acknowledge the inextricable connection between their professional actions and their personal values, assumptions, and beliefs. Understanding this, they accept responsibility to consistently examine how their personal perspectives are affecting learning for all students, especially for those who need extra support, such as newcomers who are not yet speaking English or students with emotional or physical constraints or who are living in poverty. Leaders fully commit to ensuring continuous learning — their own and others' — and find a personal/professional balance that allows them to sustain behavior that systematically demonstrates ethics, integrity, justice, and equity.

EXAMPLE INDICATORS OF PRACTICE

5A-1   Examine personal assumptions, values, and beliefs to address students' various academic, linguistic, cultural, social-emotional, physical, and economic assets and needs and promote equitable practices and access appropriate resources.

5A-2   Reflect on areas for improvement and take responsibility for change and growth.

5A-3   Engage in professional learning to be up-to-date with education research, literature, best practices, and trends to strengthen ability to lead.

5A-4   Continuously improve cultural proficiency skills and competency in curriculum, instruction, and assessment for all learners.

5A-5   Sustain personal motivation, commitment, energy, and health by balancing professional and personal responsibilities.

Leaders act upon a personal code of ethics that requires continuous reflection and learning.

Practice that is directed toward the standard	Practice that approaches the standard	Practice that meets the standard	Practice that exemplifies the standard
The administrator knows about ethical and moral issues in education and the potential consequences of related action. S/he understands that personal assumptions, values, and beliefs influence how s/he acknowledges student assets and addresses students' various academic, linguistic, cultural, social-emotional, physical, and economic needs. S/he is able and willing to reflect on personal and professional challenges in order to identify areas in need of improvement, but is inconsistent in making time to do so. The administrator realizes that it is her/his ethical responsibility to keep up to date on research and best practices that apply to increasing student learning and well-being and seeks out opportunities for professional and personal learning. S/he is searching for ways to balance professional and personal responsibilities.	The administrator reflects on and refines personal assumptions, values, and beliefs as a way to align her/his personal code of ethics with her/his professional responsibilities for addressing students' various academic, linguistic, cultural, social-emotional, physical, and economic needs and building on their assets. S/he takes responsibility for personal growth by identifying and initiating professional learning that strengthens her/his ability to promote equitable practices and access to appropriate resources for staff and for students. The administrator engages in opportunities to develop cultural proficiency skills and identify relevant research, best practices, and trends in curriculum, instruction, and assessment appropriate for supporting all students' learning and well-being. S/he initiates a plan for balancing professional and personal responsibilities so as to maintain her/his motivation, commitment, energy, and health.	The leader models self-awareness by engaging in reflective practice that results in greater insight into personal assumptions, values, and beliefs that affect her/his actions. S/he demonstrates her/his values and beliefs through personal and professional codes of ethics that promote equitable practices that address students' various academic, linguistic, cultural, social-emotional, physical, and economic needs and that build on students' assets. The leader regularly examines her/his performance, considering how personal actions affect others and influence progress toward the goal of having all students graduate ready for college and career. The leader continuously improves her/his performance by actively engaging in ongoing professional learning that incorporates research and best practices focused on standards-based curriculum, instruction, and assessment, and on cultural proficiency. The leader balances professional and personal responsibilities in order to sustain personal motivation, commitment, energy, and health.	The leader regularly analyzes her/his values and beliefs to reflect on how her/his personal and professional codes of ethics shape collaborations with students, staff, and stakeholders. The leader publicly shares her/his codes of ethics and explicitly connects them with the advocacy and actions required to implement and sustain equitable practices that address students' various academic, linguistic, cultural, social-emotional, physical, and economic needs and that build on their assets. The leader continuously improves her/his performance by capitalizing on research and best practices focused on curriculum, instruction, assessment, and culturally proficient behavior to transform teaching and learning. The leader's behaviors model a work/life balance that sustains personal motivation, commitment, energy, and health.

Education leaders make decisions, model, and behave in ways that demonstrate professionalism, ethics, integrity, justice, and equity and hold staff to the same standard.

ELEMENT 5B

Ethical Decision-Making

Leaders guide and support personal and collective actions that use relevant evidence and available research to make fair and ethical decisions.

Leaders constantly seek out and analyze relevant evidence and research in order to make fair and ethical decisions. They work alone and with others to pinpoint institutional biases and barriers stemming from sources of educational disadvantage and discrimination, such as economics, race, language, gender identification, and social-emotional or physical factors. Leaders are resolute in consistently reviewing the moral and legal consequences of their decisions and unwavering in their commitment to make the difficult decisions necessary to enact equitable outcomes for students, staff, and the community.

EXAMPLE INDICATORS
OF PRACTICE

5B-1 Consider and evaluate the potential moral and legal consequences of decisions.

5B-2 Review multiple measures of data and research on effective teaching and learning, leadership, management practices, equity, and other pertinent areas to inform decision-making.

5B-3 Identify personal and institutional biases and remove barriers that derive from economic, social-emotional, racial, linguistic, cultural, physical, gender-based, or other sources of educational disadvantage or discrimination.

5B-4 Commit to making difficult decisions in service of equitable outcomes for students, staff, and the school community.

Leaders guide and support personal and collective actions that use relevant evidence and available research to make fair and ethical decisions.

Practice that is directed toward the standard	Practice that approaches the standard	Practice that meets the standard	Practice that exemplifies the standard
The administrator is able to analyze and draw conclusions about many of the moral implications and potential legal consequences of decisions. S/he explains to staff the importance of using relevant research and evidence in making fair decisions. The administrator supports staff's access to various sources of information about effective teaching and learning, leadership, management practices, equity, and other content that contribute to making fair and ethical decisions about instruction and support services. The administrator facilitates staff discussions about personal and institutional biases that are obstacles to student learning and well-being and strategizes with them on ways to individually and collectively address those biases. The leader articulates her/his personal commitment to fair and ethical decisions and practices.	The administrator dialogues with site and district staff when considering potential moral and legal consequences of individual and site decisions. S/he regularly engages staff in examining student data and guides them in using the information appropriately and fairly. S/he supports staff to review their individual assumptions and beliefs about teaching and learning, and, then, to identify any biases institutionalized in site policies and practices. Together, s/he and staff consider these obstacles to student learning and ways to remove barriers, including those specifically related to economic, social-emotional, racial, linguistic, cultural, physical, gender, or any other sources of education disadvantage or discrimination. S/he commits to making difficult decisions in the service of equitable outcomes for students, staff, and the community.	The leader works with site and district staff and others to adopt a set of guiding criteria for considering and evaluating potential moral and legal consequences of individual and collective decisions. Together, s/he and staff consistently apply current research on effective teaching and learning, leadership, management practices, and equity, coupled with data from multiple sources, to make fair and ethical decisions. S/he coaches staff and community members to examine and address personal and institutional biases that are barriers to student learning, including those specifically related to economic, social-emotional, racial, linguistic, cultural, physical, gender, or other sources of education disadvantage or discrimination. S/he is transparent about the criteria and ethical principles applied in decision-making and honors her/his commitment to prioritize the needs of students, staff, and the school community when resolving conflicts.	The leader shares leadership with staff and community members in monitoring and updating criteria and processes for considering and evaluating potential moral and legal consequences of individual and collective decisions. With staff, along with external experts, s/he reviews pertinent existing research and collaborates with them in conducting action-research related to their own questions about effective teaching and learning, leadership, management, and equity relevant to making fair and ethical decisions on behalf of students and the community. S/he and staff escalate action that eliminates personal and institutional barriers emanating from economic, social-emotional, racial, linguistic, cultural, physical, gender, or other sources of education disadvantage or discrimination. The leader works with others to grow collective capacity and commitment to persist in making difficult decisions aimed at achieving equitable outcomes for students, staff, and the community.

Education leaders make decisions, model, and behave in ways that demonstrate professionalism, ethics, integrity, justice, and equity and hold staff to the same standard.

ELEMENT 5C

Ethical Action

Leaders recognize and use their professional influence with staff and the community to develop a climate of trust, mutual respect, and honest communication, necessary to consistently make fair and equitable decisions on behalf of all students.

Leaders engender a climate of trust by modeling transparent, respectful, and open communication when working with staff, families, and community members. In striving to have a learning site marked by ethics, integrity, justice, and equity — and in inspiring others to push toward that goal as well — leaders demonstrate the principle that students' well-being supersedes the interests of any one community member. Leaders are constantly aware of their authority and are mindful in using their influence constructively and productively in the service of students, staff, families, and community members.

EXAMPLE INDICATORS OF PRACTICE

5C-1   Communicate expectations and support for professional behavior that reflects ethics, integrity, justice, and equity.

5C-2   Use a variety of strategies to lead others in safely examining personal assumptions and respectfully challenge beliefs that negatively affect improving teaching and learning for all students.

5C-3   Encourage and inspire others to higher levels of performance, commitment, and motivation by modeling transparent and accountable behavior.

5C-4   Protect the rights and appropriate confidentiality of students, staff, and families.

5C-5   Promote understanding and follow the legal, social, and ethical use of technology among all members of the school community.

Leaders recognize and use their professional influence with staff and the community to develop a climate of trust, mutual respect, and honest communication, necessary to consistently make fair and equitable decisions on behalf of all students.

Practice that is directed toward the standard	Practice that approaches the standard	Practice that meets the standard	Practice that exemplifies the standard
The administrator recognizes that her/his role can lead to professional influence. S/he expresses the necessity of having a climate of trust, respect, and communication in order to make fair decisions for students. S/he communicates expectations that staff decisions reflect ethics, integrity, justice, and equity. The administrator guides staff in discussing assumptions and beliefs about teaching and learning that can negatively affect outcomes for students. S/he strives to be a role model for staff. S/he protects student and staff confidentiality by following legal, social, and ethical use of technology and encouraging staff to do the same.	The administrator activates her/his professional influence with staff by initiating activities that develop the climate of trust, respect, and communication needed to make fair and equitable decisions for students. The administrator communicates and supports the expectation that staff actions reflect ethics, integrity, justice, and equity. The administrator facilitates a process by which staff can safely examine any personal assumptions and beliefs about teaching and learning that negatively affect outcomes for students. The administrator sets an example for high expectations and transparent action that colleagues notice and are inspired to emulate in their own performance, commitment, and accountable behavior. The administrator protects the rights and confidentially of staff and students and promotes staff understanding of the legal, social, and ethical use of technology.	The leader uses her/his professional influence to engage staff and the community in nurturing a climate of trust, mutual respect, and honest communication that undergirds fair and equitable decisions for all students. The leader bases her/his actions on a foundation reflecting ethics, integrity, justice, and equity, and s/he communicates expectations and provides support for the same professional behavior from staff. S/he employs varied strategies to support staff and community members in safely examining their own assumptions about teaching and learning and to respectfully challenge any beliefs that undermine equitable outcomes for all students. S/he models transparent, accountable behavior to encourage staff and others to higher levels of performance, commitment, and motivation. The leader consistently protects the rights and confidentiality of students, staff, and families and guides the legal, social, and ethical use of technology.	The leader intentionally extends her/his professional influence to staff, students, and community members so that, together, they support and sustain the climate of trust, mutual respect, and honest communication needed for fair and equitable actions on behalf of all students. S/he collaborates with staff and the community to monitor and refine collective actions to reflect ethics, integrity, justice, and equity. S/he enables staff and community members to use strategies that assist them and other stakeholders in safely and regularly challenging assumptions and beliefs about teaching and learning that negatively affect actions taken on behalf of all students. The leader models, monitors, and coaches transparent and accountable behavior to lift staff, students, and community members to higher levels of performance, commitment, and motivation. S/he works with staff and other stakeholders to understand and protect student, staff, and family confidentiality, and to adhere to legal, social, and ethical technology use.

Education leaders influence political, social, economic, legal, and cultural contexts affecting education to improve education policies and practices.

Understanding and Communicating Policy

Leaders actively structure and participate in opportunities that develop greater public understanding of the education policy environment.

Leaders advance public understanding of education policy and its impact on whether all students have opportunities to learn and thrive. They are positioned to groom individuals and groups to participate in ongoing dialogue and processes that identify, shape, and respond to issues, trends, and potential changes related to the operating environments of their sites. Leaders are able to do this because they understand how political, social, and economic systems and processes affect their sites. They untangle the interrelationships among agencies to artfully apply the principles and structures of governance and policymaking in order to influence local, state, and federal policies associated with their site's goals of excellence and equity.

EXAMPLE INDICATORS OF PRACTICE

6A-1 Operate consistently within the parameters of federal, state, and local laws, policies, regulations, and statutory requirements.

6A-2 Understand and can explain the roles of school leaders, boards of education, legislators, and other key stakeholders in making education policy.

6A-3 Welcome and facilitate conversations with the local community about how to improve learning and achievement for all students, including English Learners and students needing additional support.

6A-4 Facilitate discussions with the public about federal, state, and local laws, policies, regulations, and statutory requirements affecting continuous improvement of educational programs and outcomes.

6A-5 Work with local leaders to assess, analyze, and anticipate emerging trends and initiatives and their impact on education.

Leaders actively structure and participate in opportunities that develop greater public understanding of the education policy environment.

Practice that is directed toward the standard	Practice that approaches the standard	Practice that meets the standard	Practice that exemplifies the standard
The administrator manages her/his site to comply with federal, state, and local laws and policies, following district direction. S/he invites the local community to the site to discuss how to improve education programs and student achievement for all students, including those needing extra support. In that discussion, s/he incorporates information about federal, state, and local education laws and policies. S/he knows the roles of school leaders, education boards, legislators, and other key stakeholders in making education policy. The administrator participates in district meetings to understand the district's parameters for an administrator's engagement in policy discussions and development.	The administrator, during planning and monitoring processes, discusses with staff and site governance groups the major federal, state, and local laws, regulations, and policies affecting the site and how the site operates within them. S/he understands and can explain the roles of school leaders, education boards, legislators, and other decision-makers in developing education policy. The administrator encourages the local community, and at times a broader public audience, to participate in planned activities to talk with her/him and staff about how to improve student learning and achievement for all students, including English Learners and students needing additional support. S/he uses these opportunities to elicit a broader perspective about future site and student needs.	The leader guides and supports staff and community members in operating consistently within local, state, and federal parameters. S/he structures various opportunities for staff and community to build understanding of federal, state, and local laws, policies, regulations, and statutory requirements, by hosting and facilitating conversations that explain them and how they affect education programs and outcomes for all students, including English Learners and students needing additional support. The leader uses her/his understanding of the relationships between and among school leaders, education boards, legislators, and other key stakeholders to explain policy development processes to staff and community members. The leader leverages increased public understanding of education policy to identify and address emerging trends and initiatives that affect school and district priorities and actions.	The leader shares responsibility and accountability with staff and stakeholders to operate consistently within federal, state, and local laws, regulations, and policies. The leader establishes and co-facilitates regularly scheduled study sessions and forums in which staff and stakeholders discuss continuously improving education programs and outcomes for all students, including English Learners and those needing additional support, and how federal state, and local education laws, policies, regulations, and statutory requirements relate to the site's goals. S/he engages community members in expanding their collective understanding of how the work of school leaders, education boards, legislators, and other key stakeholders connect, and s/he explores potential conflicts or agreements among agencies or stakeholders that may arise during the development of policies. Together, they analyze emerging policy trends to forecast external factors that may affect site and district goals, programs, practices, and resources.

Education leaders influence political, social, economic, legal, and cultural contexts affecting education to improve education policies and practices.

ELEMENT 6B

Professional Influence

Leaders use their understanding of social, cultural, economic, legal, and political contexts to shape policies that lead to all students graduating ready for college and career.

Leaders focus squarely on improving outcomes for student growth and well-being and also commit to influencing a range of stakeholders and policymakers to care about these outcomes. They champion principles of equity and adequacy by educating and influencing policymakers about ways to ameliorate challenges to learning and well-being that are faced by students and families, including those with specific education, linguistic, cultural, social-emotional, legal, physical, and economic needs. Leaders use their understanding of various contexts (social, cultural, economic, legal, and political) to equitably deploy resources and support services so that all students graduate ready for college and career.

EXAMPLE INDICATORS
OF PRACTICE

6B-1 Advocate for equity and adequacy in providing for students' and families' educational, linguistic, cultural, social-emotional, legal, physical, and economic needs, so that every student can meet education expectations and goals.

6B-2 Support public policies and administrative procedures that provide for present and future needs of all children and families and improve equity and excellence in education.

6B-3 Promote public policies that ensure the equitable distribution of resources and support services for all students.

ELEMENT 6B / Professional Influence

Leaders use their understanding of social, cultural, economic, legal, and political contexts to shape policies that lead to all students graduating ready for college and career.

Practice that is directed toward the standard	Practice that approaches the standard	Practice that meets the standard	Practice that exemplifies the standard
The administrator discusses with staff the education, linguistic, cultural, social-emotional, legal, physical, and economic needs of their site's students and families. S/he facilitates discussions at staff meetings to identify ways the site can work on ensuring the adequacy and equitable allocation of student resources and supports so that every student has the opportunity to meet education goals. The administrator follows public policies and procedures that are relevant to student and family needs. The administrator publicizes opportunities for staff and the broader site community to participate in planning for the equitable distribution of resources and support services.	The administrator supports staff in developing a common understanding of what the adequacy and equitable allocation of student resources and supports means at the site, and s/he discusses site issues and solutions with them, highlighting the education, linguistic, cultural, social-emotional, legal, physical, and economic needs of their students and families. S/he supports public policies and procedures that provide for the current needs of all children and families and that improve equity outcomes that lead to having every student graduate ready for college and career. The administrator engages staff and the local community in planning for the equitable distribution of resources and support services for all students.	The leader works with staff and community members to identify equitable policies and practices that address the education, linguistic, cultural, social-emotional, legal, physical, and economic needs of the site's students and families, and s/he advocates for adequacy and equitable allocation of student resources and supports. S/he supports public policies and administrative procedures intended to address present and future student and family needs and focuses attention on improving education so that all students graduate ready for college and career. The leader sponsors staff and community participation in working with her/him to promote public policies directed toward the equitable distribution of resources and support services for all students.	The leader collaborates with staff and community members to develop collective capacity to advocate for equitable actions directed toward addressing the education, linguistic, cultural, social-emotional, legal, physical, and economic needs of students and families. S/he shapes policies and procedures to actively address the present and future needs of students and families with ongoing action that results in all students graduating ready for college and career. With the community and external stakeholders, the leader promotes public policies and plans for the adequacy and equitable allocation of resources and support services for all students.

Education leaders influence political, social, economic, legal, and cultural contexts affecting education to improve education policies and practices.

ELEMENT 6C

Policy Engagement

Leaders engage with policymakers and stakeholders to collaborate on education policies focused on improving education for all students.

Leaders initiate relationships with a broad range of stakeholders in order to shape education policy that reflects a commitment to the learning and well-being of all students. They are proactive in seeking opportunities to engage in dialogue about education policy and its effect on practice. Leaders convene district, governing board, and local leaders, as well as researchers and specialists, employing their collective expertise to identify and act upon issues, trends, and changes that propel the improvement of teaching and learning.

EXAMPLE INDICATORS OF PRACTICE

6C-1 Work with the governing board, district and local leaders to influence policies that benefit students and support the improvement of teaching and learning.

6C-2 Actively develop relationships with a range of stakeholders, policymakers, and researchers to identify and address issues, trends, and potential changes that affect the context and conduct of education.

6C-3 Collaborate with community leaders and stakeholders with specialized expertise to inform district and site planning, policies, and programs that respond to cultural, economic, social, and other emerging issues.

Leaders engage with policymakers and stakeholders to collaborate on education policies focused on improving education for all students.

Practice that is directed toward the standard	Practice that approaches the standard	Practice that meets the standard	Practice that exemplifies the standard
The administrator responds to invitations from the governing board and with district and local leaders to discuss policies that benefit students and support the improvement of teaching and learning. S/he explores building relationships with stakeholders, policymakers, and researchers to identify issues and potential changes that could affect education. The administrator identifies community leaders, stakeholders, and researchers to contact when addressing cultural, economic, and social issues related to students and their families.	The administrator works with the governing board and with district and local leaders to influence local policies that benefit students and support the improvement of teaching and learning. S/he teams with stakeholders, policymakers, and researchers representing a range of interests and expertise, working with them to identify and address issues, trends, and potential changes that could affect the context and conduct of education. The administrator initiates relationships with community leaders, stakeholders, and researchers to support her/him in program planning to address cultural, economic, and social issues affecting students and their families.	The leader shares responsibility with the governing board and with district and local leaders to influence policies that benefit students and support the improvement of teaching and learning. S/he actively develops relationships with stakeholders, policymakers, and researchers, who have varied areas of interest and expertise, to identify and address issues, trends, and potential changes that could affect the context and conduct of education. The leader partners with community leaders, stakeholders, and researchers — all with identified expertise — to inform specific district and school planning, policies, and programs that address current and emerging cultural, economic, and social issues affecting students and their families.	The leader shares responsibility with the governing board and with district and local leaders to influence policies that benefit students and support the improvement of teaching and learning. S/he capitalizes on well-developed relationships with stakeholders, policymakers, and researchers who have varied areas of interest and expertise, to affect policy changes related to the most important issues and trends of education. The leader is engaged with community leaders, stakeholders, and researchers in active and ongoing collaborations to inform district and site planning, policies, and programs that respond to current and emerging cultural, economic, and social issues that affect students and their families.

Principal Evaluation Resource Collection

Developed by the California Comprehensive Center at WestEd

This **free collection** provides examples and features of effective principal evaluation systems employed by states and districts. Resources include considerations for developing local systems; examples of implementation processes and resources that support these systems; and literature reviews identifying themes and perspectives that might be useful to practitioners and policymakers working to improve district principal evaluation systems.

The collection can be useful for both research and practice purposes, providing multiple examples of current principal evaluation policies and systems. Information in this collection can help states and districts identify resources to be considered in taking appropriate next steps to evaluate school leaders, design an evaluation method, and/or buy a program or service.

Key Features of a Comprehensive Principal Evaluation System

This in-depth review of research and literature identifies 13 key features as critical in establishing a comprehensive principal evaluation system.

The Policies and Practices of Principal Evaluation: A Review of the Literature

This comprehensive literature review identifies themes and perspectives and provides insights into how to best evaluate school principals.

A Brief Overview of Principal Evaluation Literature: Implications for Selecting Evaluation Models

The brief presents highlights from *Policies and Practices of Principal Evaluation: A Review of the Literature*, a comprehensive review of principal evaluation systems.

How Six States are Implementing Principal Evaluation Systems

This brief provides policymakers and practitioners with information and web links related to principal evaluation policies and systems in six states.

An Overview of Commercially Available Principal Evaluation Resources

This brief can assist state and district leaders in making decisions about commercially available principal evaluation resources that may be useful.

How Four Districts Crafted Innovative Principal Evaluation Systems: Success Stories in Collaboration

This publication uses informal case studies to provide concrete examples of innovative and effective principal evaluation systems.

 Download these resources at **http://www.WestEd.org/principal-evaluation**